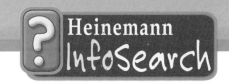

Living in a Prairie

Heinemann Library
Chicago, Illinois

Carol Baldwin

Customer Service 888-454-2279

Visit our website at www.heinemannlibrary.com

Designed by Kimberly Saar, Heinemann Library
Illustrations and maps by John Fleck
Photo research by Bill Broyles
Printed and bound in the United States by Lake Book Manufacturing, Inc.

07 06 05 04 03
10 9 8 7 6 5 4 3 2 1

Library of Congress Cataloging-in-Publication Data
Baldwin, Carol, 1943-
   Living in a prairie / Carol Baldwin.
      v. cm. -- (Living habitats)
Includes index.
Contents: What are prairies? -- Why are prairies important? -- What's green and growing on a prairie? -- What animals live on a prairie? -- What's for dinner on the prairie -- How do prairie animals get food? -- How do prairies affect people? -- How do people affect prairies? -- Earth's grasslands.
   ISBN 1-40340-841-6 (lib. bdg. : hardcover)
   1. Prairie ecology--Juvenile literature. [1. Prairie ecology. 2.Prairies. 3. Ecology.] I. Title.
   QH541.5.P7 B35 2003
   577.4'4--dc21
                              2002011354

Acknowledgments
The author and publishers are grateful to the following for permission to reproduce copyright material:
p. 4 Noboru Komine/Photo Researchers, Inc.; p. 5 Roy Attaway/Photo Researchers, Inc.; pp. 6, 8, 23 Jim Steinberg/Animals Animals; p. 7 Maslowski/Visuals Unlimited; p. 9 John Lemker/Animals Animals; p. 10 Adam Jones/Photo Researchers, Inc.; p. 11 Ted Kerasote/Photo Researchers, Inc.; p. 12 Beth Davidow/Visuals Unlimited; p. 13 Alectura Lathami/Photo Researchers, Inc.; p. 14 Tom & Pat Leeson/Photo Researchers, Inc.; p. 15 Peter Holden/Visuals Unlimited; p. 16 Ken Cole/Animals Animals; p. 17 Roger Williams Park Zoo, Providence, Rhode Island; p. 18 Tom McHugh/Photo Researchers, Inc.; p. 20 Blair Seitz/Photo Researchers, Inc.; p. 21 Inga Spence/Visuals Unlimited; p. 22 Kit Houghton/Corbis; p. 24 Scott T. Smith/Corbis; p. 25 Jack Fields/Photo Researchers, Inc.; p. 26 Dorothea Lange/Library of Congress; p. 27 National Wildlife Federation

Cover photograph: Richard T. Nowitz/Corbis

Some words are shown in bold, **like this**. You can find out what they mean by looking in the glossary.

Contents

1 What Are Prairies?

In front of you is a huge piece of land with lots and lots of grass. It reaches as far as your eyes can see. This **habitat** is a grassland.

Prairies are a kind of grassland

There are two main kinds of grasslands. Savannas are grasslands in warm or hot climates. Savannas occur in Africa, Australia, South America, and India. They have a few trees scattered about. Prairies are cool, or **temperate,** grasslands. Temperate grasslands have hot summers and cold winters. They don't get as much rain as savannas do.

Prairies can have different names

Cool grasslands are called prairies in North America. But they are called pampas in South America and steppes in Eurasia. In South Africa, they are called veld, and in Australia they are called bush or downs.

Not all grasslands are flat. These hilly grasslands are in Mongolia.

Prairies have different climates

Summer temperatures in prairies can be more than 100 °F (38 °C). Winter temperatures can be as low as −40 °F (−40 °C). Prairies receive between 10 and 30 inches (25 and 76 centimeters) of rain each year. Most of the rain falls in late spring and early summer. In winter, it often snows.

The Tallgrass Prairie Reserve in Oklahoma has a few trees. This is normal for tallgrass prairies.

The height of a prairie's grasses depends on how much rain a grassland gets. Grasslands that get more rain have taller grasses. In the United States, tallgrass prairie lies in the eastern part of the Midwest. The yearly rainfall is about 30 inches. Grasses there often grow to be five feet (one and one-half meters) tall.

The midgrass prairie lies in the middle part of the Midwest. It gets 15 to 25 inches (38 to 64 centimeters) of rain. These grasses grow 2 to 3 feet ($\frac{1}{2}$ to 1 meter) tall. The shortgrass prairie is in the western part of the Midwest. It gets only about 10 inches of rain. These grasses grow less than 2 feet tall.

Why Are Prairies Important?

Prairies are important to many living things. People, plants, and animals all use prairies.

Prairie land provides food for people

Nearly three-fourths of the world's food is grown on land that used to be prairies. Almost all of the wild grasslands have been turned into farms and **grazing** land. Ninety-nine out of every 100 acres of wild tallgrass prairie are gone.

Soil in tallgrass and midgrass prairies is very **fertile.** It's good for growing wheat, corn, and other grains. People use shortgrass prairies for grazing cattle and sheep. These animals are used as food.

Sod busting

Ground covered with grass is sometimes called sod. Many early settlers plowed this treeless land. So the early farmers in the Midwest were called sod busters. Plowing the prairies was called sod busting.

North America has some of the largest farms in the world. These wheat fields used to be prairies.

Many grassland birds, like this horned lark, build their nests on the ground.

Prairies are home to plants

There are more than 9,000 different kinds of grasses. Different grasses grow in different grasslands. Bluestem grasses grow in the tallgrass prairies of North America. Buffalo grass grows in shortgrass prairies. Pampas grass grows in South America.

Natural grasslands often have many kinds of flowers. Wild tulips grow in the Eurasian steppes. Prairie buttercups grow in the tallgrass prairies of North America. Some trees grow along streams or rivers running through prairies.

Prairies are home to animals

Insects, such as grasshoppers, live in prairies. Many kinds of birds live in grasslands. There are usually only a few trees to nest in. Birds like meadowlarks make nests in the grass. Prairie chickens lay their eggs on the ground. Grasslands also are home to many large and small animals. Tiny deer mice live alongside huge bison.

What's Green and Growing in a Prairie?

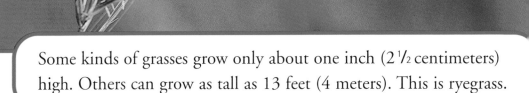

Some kinds of grasses grow only about one inch (2 ½ centimeters) high. Others can grow as tall as 13 feet (4 meters). This is ryegrass.

In a grassland **habitat,** the main plants are grasses. But other plants grow there as well.

Grass plants

Grasses have slim, hollow stems. Their leaves are straight and narrow. Their many small roots grow matted together below the soil. The flowers of grass plants are feathery tufts at the top of the stem. Grass flowers do not have petals. Seeds form from the flowers. Inside each seed is a grain. People and animals use these grains for food.

Most plants grow from their tips. But grasses grow from their base, or bottom. When **grazing** animals bite off the tops of grass plants, the grass grows out again. This is also why your lawn grows back after you mow it.

Annual grasses

Some kinds of grasses sprout, make seeds, and die in a year or less. These are **annual** grasses. Annual grasses make many seeds. These tough seeds may lie in the soil or be blown away by the wind. The seeds sprout when the next rains come. Annual grasses rot when they die. They add **nutrients** back into the prairie soil. This makes the soil **fertile.**

Perennial grasses

Other kinds of grasses keep growing year after year. These are **perennial** grasses. They produce seeds, but they also reproduce by sending long stems along or under the ground. New plants, or shoots, grow from these stems. Soon, the soil is full of grass roots from these plants. The roots help hold the soil in place. They also hold water in the soil. New grass shoots grow each time animals feed on the grasses.

This big bluestem is one kind of perennial prairie grass.

9

During spring and summer, many colorful flowers bloom among the grasses of this Texas prairie. These are bluebonnets.

Prairie flowers

Natural grasslands often have many kinds of flowers. They are **adapted** to getting and keeping water. Many, such as the scarlet globemallow, have long **taproots** that go deep into the soil to get water.

Some prairie flowers are covered with silvery or white hairs. The prairie star has leaves that are covered with fine hairs. Cream cups have both hairy leaves and stems. The small pasque flower is covered with hairs. Hairs reflect some of the sun's rays. They also protect plants from the drying wind.

Black-eyed susans grow from one to three feet (one-third to one meter) tall. They have yellow flower heads with dark brown centers. The leaves are long and fuzzy. The plant stems have tiny **bristles** that keep insect pests from climbing the plants.

Compass plants are tall, flowering plants. Bright yellow flowers bloom at the tops of stems that can be twelve feet (four meters) tall. The plant got its name because its leaves point upward, with their edges pointing north and south.

Trees and shrubs

Most trees and shrubs need more rain than a grassland gets. But a few small trees and shrubs, like prairie crabapples, can grow in grasslands. Prairie crabapples grow in the tallgrass prairies of the United States. In North America, you

Trees and shrubs usually grow only along streams in grasslands.

might see other trees and shrubs growing along a stream or river in the prairie. Here, their roots can get enough water to grow. Box elder and wild plum trees often grow along streams in prairies.

Prairie shrubs are also adapted to get and keep water. Some, such as yuccas, have waxy coverings to hold in water. Others have dew-trapping hairs. Cactuses, such as prickly pears, also grow on the shortgrass prairie. They store water in their thick pads.

What Animals Live in a Prairie?

The color of a grasshopper lets it blend into its grassland **habitat**.

Many animals live year-round on the prairie. Others just pass through.

Insects

Prairie plants attract many kinds of insects. Monarch butterflies lay their eggs on milkweed plants. When the eggs hatch, the **larvae** eat the milkweed leaves. Adult butterflies feed on **nectar** from flowers. Many other kinds of butterflies also live in grasslands.

Grasshoppers use the grasses for food and shelter. Locusts are a kind of grasshopper. Sometimes they move in large swarms, or groups, of millions. They travel across the grasslands eating the plants.

Termites live in the pampas of South America. They build huge nests. The nests are brown mounds that stick up above the grass. More than one million termites can live in a nest. They store chopped pieces of dry grass in the mounds as food.

This Australian brush turkey has stuck his leg down into his nest to check the temperature.

Birds

Many birds live in **temperate** grasslands all the time. But some stop only to rest and feed as they **migrate** from **habitats** farther north or south.

Australian brush turkeys lay eggs in nests made of rotting plants. The male covers the eggs. Heat from the sun and the rotting plants **incubates** the eggs. When the eggs hatch, the chicks dig their way out and run away.

Quails spend most of their time on the ground. There, they find leaves and insects to eat. But they can and do fly. Quails of the northern steppes migrate south in winter.

Most cranes live in wetlands. They have long, strong bills to feed on fish and frogs. But the demoiselle crane of the steppes has a short bill. This allows it to grab and eat insects and grass seeds.

As many as 35 prairie dogs can live on one acre (about one-half hectare).

Animals that live underground

There aren't many places to hide on the prairie. So it's safer to live underground. Many prairie animals live in **burrows.** Burrows also stay warmer in winter and cooler in summer.

On the North American prairies, you might see mounds of packed dirt. The mounds mark the entrances to prairie dog burrows. These animals live in large groups, called colonies or towns. Several "rooms" extend off of each burrow. Burrows give prairie dogs places to sleep, raise young, and find shelter.

Hairy-nosed wombats are **nocturnal** animals that live in Australia's grasslands. They spend most of their days in their burrows. At night, wombats come out to search for food.

Bobaks, a type of marmot, live on the Eurasian steppes. In fall, they move to winter burrows where they **hibernate.**

? Did you know?

The pronghorn antelope, sometimes called the prairie ghost, can reach a top speed of about 60 miles (40 kilometers) per hour.

Animals that roam the prairies

Many animals move around the grasslands.
Most of the time they are looking for food.
Some animals look for plants to eat. Bison

Wallabies roam the Australian bush, grazing on grasses and shrubs. This one has a baby, called a joey, in its pouch.

and pronghorns roam the North American prairies. Pampas deer wander the grasslands of South America. Onagers travel the Eurasian steppes. And wallabies and kangaroos hop around Australia's bush.

Some animals search for other animals to eat. Coyotes of the prairie and dingoes of the bush look for small animals. Rough-legged hawks spend the winters hunting in the grasslands of North America and Eurasia. Like other hawks, they hunt during the day. Most owls are nocturnal and hunt at night. But the short-eared owl of the prairie is **diurnal.** It often hunts for mice during the day.

5 What's for Dinner in the Prairie?

All life, in all **habitats,** begins with plants. Animals eat the plants. Other animals eat the plant-eaters.

Plants

Plants make, or produce, their own food. They are called **producers.** Plants such as grasses and wildflowers are producers that grow in grasslands. They make food from carbon dioxide gas in the air and water from their roots. Plants need energy to change the carbon dioxide and water into sugars. The energy comes from sunlight. This process is called **photosynthesis.**

Badgers feed on birds, snakes, insects, worms, fruits, and plant roots.

Animals

Animals are called **consumers** because they eat, or consume, food. Some grassland animals, such as grasshoppers, voles, and bison, eat only plants. These animals are **herbivores.** Other animals, such as badgers and coyotes, eat both plants and animals. They are **omnivores.** Still others, such as rattlesnakes and barn owls, eat only animals. They are called **carnivores.**

The clean-up crew

Other kinds of consumers feed on dead plants and animals and their waste. They are called **decomposers. Bacteria, molds,** and some beetles are decomposers. Without them, dead plants and animals would pile up everywhere.

Carrion beetles feed on dead animals. Adult beetles lay their eggs on a dead animal. When their **larvae** hatch from the eggs, they have food to eat. American burying beetles bury the bodies of small animals. The parent beetles use the dead animal to feed their young. They are found in Kansas, Nebraska, and Oklahoma.

Decomposers break down **nutrients** stored in dead plants and animals. They put the nutrients back into the soil, air, and water. Plants use the nutrients to help them grow.

American burying beetles can smell a dead mouse two miles (three kilometers) away.

Red kites feed on birds, snakes, and the bodies of already dead animals. They live in Europe and Asia and are an endangered species.

Some animals hunt other animals. Other animals **scavenge** or **forage.**

Hunting

Animals that hunt and kill other animals for food are **predators.** Bull snakes hunt and eat deer mice and many kinds of birds. Animals that predators eat are called **prey.** Deer mice are prey animals that eat seeds. But they also hunt and eat grasshoppers. So sometimes they are predators.

Scavenging

Red kites are birds from Europe. They are predators. They hunt and eat rats, birds, and other animals. But red kites are also grassland **scavengers.** Scavengers are animals that eat the bodies of animals that are already dead.

Foragers

Some animals, such as bison and onagers, **forage.** They move about, sometimes in groups, to search for food. They will travel great distances to find new supplies of food.

Planning the menu

The path that shows who eats what is a **food chain.** All living things are parts of food chains.

Coyote

Short-Eared Owl

Deer Mouse

Bull Snake

Dead Deer Mouse

Grasshopper

Vole

Grasshopper Sparrow

Burying Beetle

Grasses and Seeds

Wildflowers and other plants

In a food web, an arrow is drawn from "dinner," or prey, and points to the "diner," or predator.

In the North American prairies, grasshoppers eat grasses. Deer mice eat grasshoppers. And bull snakes eat the deer mice.

Another prairie food chain includes grasses, voles, and short-eared owls. A third food chain includes grass seeds, deer mice, and burying beetles. All the food chains that are connected in a prairie make up a **food web.** If all the deer mice died, the snakes, coyotes, and owls might not have enough food.

People use the seeds of grasses like wheat.

Without the **fertile** soils of grasslands, we could not feed Earth's people. We also use other prairie resources.

People learned to plant and use grasses

Early people were hunters and gatherers, who moved around looking for food. They found some grasses that were good to eat. When they began to plant seeds of these grasses, they settled in one place and became farmers.

Thousands of years later, modern farmers cleared acres of grasslands. They often did this by burning the plants. Then they planted grasses such as wheat and barley. Wheat was ground into flour to make bread. Barley was used as animal food. Farmers learned to use grass stems to make baskets and thatched roofs on houses. The invention of the plow made farming easier.

? Did you know?

Prairie grass and dirt once provided homes for people. They built houses with clods of sod because there were no trees.

Grasses help feed people

Grasses are the main source of food for people all over the world. Of the fifteen major crops that feed people, ten are grasses. These include wheat, corn, oats, rye, and barley that grow in **temperate** grasslands.

In many countries, farmers now have machines to help them. Tractors pull machines that help them plant many rows of crops at one time. Farmers also use **combines.** These big machines cut the crops and separate the straw or stems from the grains. Then the combine puts the grain into bags.

You eat foods made from grasses grown on farms. Wheat is used to make breads and other baked goods, pastas, and cereals. Corn is used to make cooking oil, cereals, and flour. Rye flour is used to make bread.

The fertile soil of tallgrass and midgrass prairies makes the land good for growing food crops.

21

About half the pampas in Argentina is used for grazing cattle.

Grasslands help feed animals

Many of the grasses grown in **temperate** grasslands are made into animal feed. Barley, rye, oats, and corn are used as animal feed.

In shortgrass prairies, animals **graze** on the grasses. In the prairies of North America, ranchers raise cattle and sheep.

Large cattle and sheep ranches take up most of the drier land in the pampas of South America. Ranchers sink deep wells to get water for their animals. Windmills pump the water to the surface.

In the Eurasian steppes, herders raise sheep, goats, camels, and **yaks.** The herders move their animals from place to place every few weeks. That way the animals don't eat the grasses too far down the stems.

Millions of sheep and cattle graze on the grasslands of Australia. Australian cattle and sheep ranches are some of the world's largest.

Fuels and minerals from the prairies

Many temperate grasslands contain fuels and **minerals** that people use. Some parts of the Eurasian steppes have deposits of oil, coal, and minerals such as iron ore.

The veld of South Africa has many minerals. Half of the world's gold is mined there. Copper, chrome, magnesium, and uranium are other minerals mined in the veld. Diamonds and other gems are also found there.

North American prairies have oil deep under the ground. Oil is first pumped to the surface. Then it is sent through pipes to **refineries.** There it is made into fuels for cars, trucks, and airplanes.

Ethanol is a fuel made mostly from corn. It can be used in cars and trucks. Four out of every ten cars in Brazil runs on pure ethanol.

This oil well is one of more than 100 wells on the Tallgrass Prairie Reserve in Oklahoma. The mineral rights are owned by the Osage Tribe. The reserve is managed by the Nature Conservancy.

Every year more and more people use the world's grasslands. In some places, few natural grasslands are left.

Farming and grazing the prairies

About one-fourth of Earth's land used to be natural grasslands. Then people started to change the grasslands. Many grasslands were plowed and changed into farms. In the steppes of eastern Europe, large areas of grassland are now used to grow wheat and other grains.

On one side of this fence, the grass has been protected from grazing animals. On the other side, the affects of overgrazing can be seen.

Today, there is little natural grassland left in North America. Only one acre (almost one-half hectare) of tallgrass prairie out of every hundred remains. Instead, farmers grow wheat and corn on most of this land. Ranchers **graze** cattle on western grasslands. They often fence large herds of cattle in one area. This causes **overgrazing** because the grass may not have time to grow back each year. Then the grasses die.

Harming prairie wildlife

Many kinds of plants and animals once lived on natural grasslands. Over time, many of the large grassland animals were killed. North American bison once numbered about 60 million. Then, settlers began to hunt them. Bison almost became **extinct.** Today, a few thousand bison live mostly in parks. Large herds of wild horses used to live on the steppes. When people started grazing sheep and goats, most of the horses died because they couldn't find food. Today, these horses are extinct in the wild. A few small herds live in zoos and in reserves.

When people farm the land, they destroy wild plants. Many animals need the plants for food. Farmers also spray **chemicals** on their crops to kill insects. Without insects, many birds and small animals can't find enough food. The grassland **food webs** can be destroyed.

These airplanes, called crop dusters, are spraying crops with chemicals. The chemicals used to kill insects can also harm birds that eat insects.

Growing cities

Another danger to grasslands is cities. Cities have expanded into the grasslands as people have built more houses, factories, roads, and railroads.

The death of a prairie

Grass roots hold water and help hold the soil together. When animals eat too much of the grass, the soil becomes bare. Grass roots can die. Then rain can wash away the soil and wind can blow the soil away. This is called **erosion.**

In the 1930s, a large part of the United States had a **drought.** Too little rain fell. The dry soil turned to dust. It blew away in the wind. Huge dust storms carried the soil hundreds of miles. The area affected the most became known as the Dust Bowl.

The Dust Bowl covered parts of Texas, Oklahoma, Kansas, and Colorado.

This restored prairie is on a 200-acre (81-hectare) farm in Hartford, Iowa.

Saving prairies

In prairies where cattle and sheep are raised, some ranchers use controlled grazing. They move the animals from place to place. This keeps the animals from **overgrazing** the grasses and gives the grasses time to grow back. Controlled grazing helps the plants and the animals that need them.

Some damaged grasslands are being **restored.** Seeds of **native** prairie plants are collected from other areas. They are planted in land that used to be a prairie. In some restored prairies, the animals have returned. Meadowlarks, falcons, coyotes, and foxes can once again be seen.

Some farmers are also restoring parts of their farms to native prairies. The farm owners share seeds from their plants with neighbors who also want to restore prairies.

Fact File

Grasslands of the World

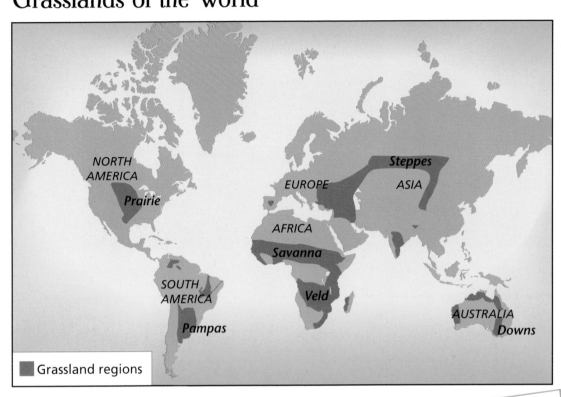

NORTH
AMERICA

Prairie

EUROPE

Steppes

ASIA

AFRICA

Savanna

SOUTH
AMERICA

Veld

AUSTRALIA

Pampas

Downs

■ Grassland regions

Many prairie plants grow better if a fire burns them every year or two. Native Americans burned prairies because they knew the young, green plants would attract buffalo and other game animals. Lightning also set the plants on fire. But fire departments and government agencies fight fires. This protects homes and businesses nearby, but it is bad for the prairies. Now, some conservation organizations and even government agencies burn prairies on purpose to save them.

Fire stops bushes and trees from growing over prairie grasses and wildflowers. Some plant seeds, like those of the lupine, will not grow at all unless they can get very hot from a fire.

Earth's Grasslands

Name	Climate	Location	Facts
prairie	temperate	central United States and southern Canadian provinces	The largest prairie dog town was in Texas. It was 100 miles (161 kilometers) wide and 250 miles (400 kilometers) long. About 400 million animals lived in it.
pampas	temperate	Argentina, Brazil and Uruguay in South America	A tall, feathery grass called pampas grass used to be the main plant until farmers and ranchers changed the land.
campos	tropical	Brazil and Paraguay in South America	Campos have hot, dry summers. When rains come, there are often floods.
veld	temperate	Southeastern Africa	Veld is a Dutch word that means field.
savanna	tropical	Central Africa	Large areas of the savanna are protected as parks for African wildlife.
steppes	temperate	Eastern Europe to eastern Asia	Large caravans used to travel across the steppes from China taking spices, cloth, and other goods to sell in Europe.
bush	temperate	Southern Australia	Twenty-four rabbits brought to Australia in 1859 multiplied to more than 200 million. They have destroyed much of the grassland.

Glossary

adapted changed to live under certain conditions

annual plant that lives only for one year

bacteria living things too small to be seen except with a microscope

bristle short, stiff hair of an animal or plant

burrow hole dug in the ground by animals for shelter

carnivore animal that eats only other animals

chemical substance that can change when mixed with another substance

combine machine used in harvesting crops

consumer living thing that needs plants for food

decomposer consumer that puts nutrients from dead plants and animals back into the soil, air, and water

diurnal active during the day

drought long period of time without rain

ethanol alcohol made from grains such as corn. Ethanol can be used as a fuel.

erosion movement of soil and rocks by water, wind, or ice

extinct no longer living on Earth

fertile able to produce crops or plants easily

food chain path that shows who eats what in a habitat

food web group of connected food chains in a habitat

forage wander about in search of food

graze feed on grass. Cattle and sheep are grazing animals.

habitat place where a plant or animal lives

herbivore animal that eats only plants

hibernate spend the winter in a state in which an animal's breathing, heart rate, and body temperature is greatly reduced

incubate keep eggs warm in order to hatch them

larvae (one is a larva) young of insects

migrate move from one place to another with the change of seasons

mineral certain materials dug from the earth by mining. Gold, iron, and diamonds are minerals.

mold living thing that uses dead plants and animals for food. Molds are decomposers.

native born, grown, or produced in a certain place

nectar sweet liquid found in many flowers

nocturnal active at night

nutrient material that is needed for growth of a plant or animal

omnivore animal that eats plants and animals

overgraze animals eat so much grass in one place that the grasses begin to die

perennial plant that lives for more than two years

photosynthesis process by which green plants trap the sun's energy and use it to change carbon dioxide and water into sugars

predator animal that hunts and eats other animals

prey animal that is hunted and eaten by other animals

producer living thing that can use sunlight to make its own food

refinery place where oil is made into other products such as gasoline

restore make something that has been changed look the way it used to look

scavenge feed on the bodies of dead animals

scavenger animal that eats the bodies of animals that are already dead

taproot main root growing downward with smaller roots growing out from it

temperate climate with warm or hot summers and cool or cold winters

yak kind of wild ox with a shaggy coat

More Books to Read

Fowler, Allan. *Lands of Grass*. Danbury, Conn.: Children's Press, 2000.

Gray, Susan H. *Grasslands.* Minneapolis, Minn.: Compass Point Books, 2001.

Ormsby, Alison. *The Prairie*. Salt Lake City, Utah: Benchmark Books, 1999.

Wilkins, Sally. *Grasslands*. Mankato, Minn.: Bridgestone Books, 2001.

Index

Helen Keller Elementary School
1806 Bond Street
Green Bay, Wisconsin 54303

Living in a

Prairie

When is a grassland not a prairie? When it's a pampas in South America, a veld in South Africa, the downs in Australia, or the steppes in Asia. In *Living in a Prairie,* you will learn that prairies are found in cool climates, and savannas in Africa are hot grasslands.

The **Living Habitats** series will show you how people and animals live in prairies and other grasslands. Learn what kinds of animals live in grasslands. See the adaptations they have to find food and shelter. Find out which plants grow well in different types of grasslands. Understand how people use prairies. Learn how prairies sometimes control how people live. Prairies and other grasslands are not empty miles of open land. They are exciting places for all life forms.

Heinemann

U.S. $6.95
CAN. $10.50

ISBN 140343225-2
9 781403 432254
90000

UN-518-976